Catalan S Recipes

A Cookbook of Catalan Region Spanish Dish Ideas!

Table of Contents

Introduction 4

Breakfast is not always eaten in Catalan households, but here are a few of the most popular breakfast recipes from the region… 6

    1 – Potato Pancake 7

    2 – Catalan Tomato Toast 10

    3 – Broken Eggs with Ham Potato 12

    4 – Escalivada 15

    5 – Catalan Paella 17

    6 – Catalan Cod Fish Esqueixad 20

    7 – Spanish Tortilla 22

    8 – Catalan Fish Stew - Suquet de Peix 25

    9 – Spanish-Style Chicken 28

    10 – Romesco Sauce 30

    11 – Broiled Mackerel 32

    12 – Catalan Calçots 34

    13 – Spanish Potatoes 36

    14 – Garbanzo Beans with Spinach 38

    15 – Catalan Bell Pepper Stew 40

    16 – Tuna Avocado Tapas 43

    17 – Catalan Squid and Rice 45

    18 – Sea Bass in Vinaigrette 48

19 – Catalan Pasta Paella 50

20 – Spanish Sausage Chicken 53

21 – Fried Artichokes 56

22 – Sherry Garlic Shrimp 59

23 – Catalan Spinach 61

24 – Catalan Vegetable Garlic Soup 63

25 – Lobster Rice 66

Like most European regions, Catalan has their own scrumptious desserts – try one soon! 69

26 – Catalan Churros 70

27 – Mel i Mató 73

28 – Crumble Cakes 75

29 – Crema Catalana 78

30 – Chocolate Turrón 81

Conclusion *84*

Introduction

How interesting can your meals be if you integrate the ingredients and recipes of Catalan into your home cooking?

Will you be able to source the ingredients locally that are integral to their dishes?

The gastronomic delicacies offered by the Catalonia region of Spain lead many people to visit the area, and her capital Barcelona, even more often than they might otherwise. It's natural to enjoy the seafood, cheeses and meats of the area. But there is much more than that to Catalan cuisine.

The area around Barcelona is internationally renowned for its food and its unique culture of eating. New chefs are making their name in the area, and you can find most ingredients in your local area, when you wish to try your hand at cooking Catalan cuisine.

Catalonia is found on the Mediterranean coast, and this gives it a varied and generous selection of intriguing ingredients. Seafood is found in abundance, as are vegetables like artichokes, mushrooms and aubergines. The mountainous areas of the region offer rich grazing for sheep and pigs, bringing more food options to the table.

It's not at all unusual to have meat and seafood in some of the same dishes in Catalan cuisine. They make the best use of the ingredients available and create some of the tastiest combinations you may find. Turn the page, and let's start cooking Catalan style…

Breakfast is not always eaten in Catalan households, but here are a few of the most popular breakfast recipes from the region...

1 – Potato Pancake

This is a unique version of Spanish omelet. It includes onions, which not all people use. It's easy to make and you can serve it as a simple breakfast or a dish for a dinner party.

Makes 4 Servings

Cooking + Prep Time: 1 1/4 hour

Ingredients:

- 2 lbs. potatoes
- Salt, kosher, as desired
- Pepper, ground, as desired
- 8 eggs, large
- 1 onion, medium

- Oil, olive

Instructions:

1. Peel potatoes. Rinse them in cold running water.

2. Slice potatoes thinly. Pat slices till dry. Place in large sized bowl, season as desired and mix thoroughly.

3. Heat 1/2" of oil in large fry pan over med-low. When oil has heated, add potatoes. You can add additional oil if you need to, so all potatoes are covered.

4. Cook potatoes for 18-20 minutes on low heat. As they cook, beat eggs in large sized bowl. Season as desired.

5. Slice onion thinly. Fry on low heat in separate pan for 12-20 minutes, till they start caramelizing. Stir them often. When they have caramelized, drain excess oil from onions. Add them to egg mixture.

6. After potatoes have fried for about 20 minutes, remove with slotted spoon into strainer. Allow excess oil to drip off as they cool.

7. After several minutes, add potatoes to egg mixture. Combine well.

8. Allow the new mixture to sit for 15-20 minutes or so.

9. In pan used for potatoes, remove oil. Add egg mixture on med-low.

10. Cook eggs for six to eight minutes each side on low heat.

11. When bottom has cooked well and you're ready to flip tortilla, flip it from the pan onto a large plate. If it's messy, that's normal, don't worry about it. Allow to cool a bit and then serve.

2 – Catalan Tomato Toast

This dish is quite versatile, eaten as breakfast but also at any other time you might crave it. Choose only the best produce and other ingredients to make the best meal.

Makes 10 Servings

Cooking + Prep Time: 35 minutes

Ingredients:

- 1 x 8" round sourdough
- 2 crossways-halved garlic cloves, large

- 3 or 4 crossways-halved ripe tomatoes, small
- 3 to 4 tbsp. of oil, olive
- Salt, coarse, as desired

Instructions:

1. Prepare your grill for med-hot heat level. Heat charcoal to medium.

2. Slice the bread in 3/4" slices.

3. Work in small batches of three to four slices. Grill the bread on oiled rack of grill. Turn once and grill till you see grill marks. Remove the bread from grill. Rub one side of slices with cut side of 1/2 garlic clove. Rub with slice side of 1/2 tomato. Allow bread to absorb most pulp. Discard remainder of tomato halves and garlic.

4. Brush the bread with olive oil. Sprinkle using coarse salt. Serve promptly.

3 – Broken Eggs with Ham Potato

Huevos rotos (broken eggs) is a popular dish in all areas of Spain, including Catalonia. It's a very simple combination of fried eggs, sausage and fried potatoes, eaten at breakfast or any time you like.

Makes 4 Servings

Cooking + Prep Time: 35 minutes

Ingredients:

- 1/2 onion, large
- 5 potatoes, medium

- To fry: 16 ounces of oil, olive
- 4 ounces of Serrano ham or Spanish chorizo
- 5 eggs, large

Instructions:

1. Peel, then chop 1/2 of onion. Sauté in several tbsp. oil. When onions have become transparent and soft, remove from pan. Set aside on plate.

2. Peel potatoes and slice them lengthways, then into the shape of French fries. Heat oil in large sized fry pan on med. heat. Salt potatoes. Fry in large pan.

3. When potatoes have cooked, remove from pan. Divide into four bowls. Keep warm.

4. Slice chorizo or sausage. Pour 1 tbsp. oil into small fry pan. Sauté sausage. Remove it and set it aside.

5. Sprinkle sautéed onions and sausage over bowls of fried potatoes.

6. Fry eggs in sunny side up method in a bit of extra oil in same pan used for sausage. Place one or two eggs in each bowl. Serve while hot, with bread.

There are all kinds of Catalan recipes for lunch, dinner, side dishes and appetizers. Try one of these truly unique recipes soon!

4 – Escalivada

This traditional dish from the Catalan countryside is sometimes referred to as grilled salad. The name refers to the dish being cooked in ashes, which means in the embers of a real wood fire.

Makes 4-6 Servings

Cooking + Prep Time: 45 minutes

Ingredients:

- 4 eggplants, medium
- 4 red peppers, large

- 4 onions, small
- 2 cloves of garlic
- Salt, kosher
- Oil, olive

Instructions:

1. Wash peppers and eggplants well.

2. Prepare sheet pan for oven. Place whole peppers on tray. Cut eggplants into halves. Cut tomatoes and onions into quarters. Dice garlic.

3. Place veggies on tray. Get them a bit wet with oil. Salt as desired.

4. Place tray on med. height in oven. Allow veggies to cook till done.

5. Remove red peppers. Wrap in foil. Leave in foil for 15-20 minutes, to sweat. This **Makes** skin removal easier. After you remove skin, slice peppers.

6. Remove skin from eggplants.

7. Display veggies as desired and serve.

5 – Catalan Paella

Once your family knows you can make this recipe, expect to be asked to prepare it often. It has true Spanish flavor and has been made in Catalan cuisine for generations.

Makes 6 Servings

Cooking + Prep Time: 1 1/4 hour

Ingredients:

- 1 1/4 lb. of chicken thighs
- 1/2 cup of oil, olive
- 1/2 cup of diced onions
- 2 chopped garlic cloves

- 1/2 diced bell pepper, green
- 1/2 diced bell pepper, red
- 1/4 lb. of calamari rings
- 1/4 lb. of peeled, de-veined shrimp, small
- 1 tsp. of salt, kosher
- 2 tsp. of saffron threads
- 1 x 14-oz. can of tomatoes, crushed
- 1/2 cup of peas, sweet
- 3 cups of rice, long grain
- 6 cups of water, filtered
- 6 scrubbed clams in the shell, large
- 6 shrimp in the shell, jumbo
- 6 sea scallops, large
- 6 lemon wedges, fresh

Instructions:

1. Heat the oil in large skillet on med-high till it starts smoking. Place chicken in skillet with the skin side facing down in oil. Sear till both sides are golden brown in color, about five minutes or so. Set chicken aside.

2. Add and stir garlic and onions into skillet. Cook till onions have turned translucent and become softened, about one or two minutes.

3. Add bell peppers, small shrimp and calamari and cook for two more minutes.

4. Add and stir water, rice, peas, tomatoes, saffron and salt in till combined well. Add the chicken and allow to simmer for 12-15 minutes on med-high. Stir frequently so rice won't stick.

5. Nestle jumbo shrimp and clams into rice decoratively. Reduce the heat down to med-low. Cover pan and allow to simmer for 10-12 minutes.

6. Place scallops in paella and cover pan again. Continue to simmer till scallops are opaque and firm, and rice becomes tender. Use lemon wedges to garnish and serve.

6 – Catalan Cod Fish Esqueixad

This is a very traditional Catalan recipe. They use cod in many ways, and it is in this one that the fish's flavor is accentuated most perfectly, for many diners.

Makes 4 Servings

Cooking + Prep Time: 25 minutes

Ingredients:

- 1 lb. of cod, salt – soaked for six hours, then rinsed and patted dry
- 1 green pepper, small
- 1 red pepper, small

- 4 ripe tomatoes, firm
- 15-18 olives, black
- 1 onion, medium
- 1 garlic clove
- Oil, olive
- Salt, kosher
- Pepper, ground
- Vinegar, red wine

Instructions:

1. Shred cod in pieces using your fingers. Place in serving type dish.

2. Chop bell peppers and onion finely. Cut tomatoes into halves. Grate tomato pulp. Mince garlic.

3. Throw all prepared ingredients on plate with fish. Toss well. Top with olives. Dress with vinegar and oil. Season as desired. Toss again. Serve.

7 – Spanish Tortilla

This dish is easily prepared and always pleases guests. It was originally made without greens, but nowadays, chives or parsley are found more commonly in the dish.

Makes 4 Servings

Cooking + Prep Time: 55 minutes

Ingredients:

- 1 tbsp. of oil, olive + extra as needed
- 2 peeled, thinly sliced potatoes, large
- Salt, kosher, as desired
- Pepper, ground, as desired
- 1/4 tsp. of paprika, smoked, +/- as desired
- 1 thinly sliced Spanish onion, sweet
- 6 eggs, large
- 1 tsp. of oil, olive
- 1 bunch of chopped parsley, fresh
- 1 tbsp. of oil, olive

Instructions:

1. Preheat oven to 350F.

2. In oven-proof skillet on med. heat, heat 1 tbsp. oil till it is shimmering. Place potatoes in hot oil. Season as desired. Sprinkle with paprika.

3. Pan fry potatoes, tossing and stirring occasionally, till they begin to soften, or about eight minutes. Stir in onion. Stir occasionally while cooking till onion and potatoes are browned slightly and onion has become translucent, 10-12

minutes more or so. Remove skillet from heat. Let it cool for five to seven minutes.

4. Beat eggs with 1 tsp. oil in large sized bowl. Add parsley and stir. Add onion-potato mixture and combine lightly.

5. Heat 1 tbsp. oil in skillet on med. heat till it is shimmering. Spoon potato-egg mixture gently into skillet. Reduce the heat down to med-low. Shake skillet several times, releasing omelet from bottom of skillet.

6. Slide skillet in preheated oven. Bake till omelet has puffed up and top is a golden brown in color, about five to seven minutes. Toothpick inserted in middle of omelet should come back clean. Slice omelet into pieces. Serve while hot.

8 – Catalan Fish Stew - Suquet de Peix

"Suquet de Peix" translates to "fish stew" in the language of Catalonia. It has been served in the region for many years. There are many variations, and this is a favorite.

Makes 4-6 Servings

Cooking + Prep Time: 35 minutes

Ingredients:

For picada sauce

- 1 3/4 oz. of almonds, whole
- 2 slices of bread, stale
- 3 or 4 tbsp. of parsley, flat leaf, with removed stems
- 2 garlic cloves
- 1 to 2 tbsp. of vinegar, red wine
- 2 to 4 tbsp. of oil, olive

For stew

- 1 garlic clove
- 1 onion
- 3 large tomatoes, ripe
- 1 pound of potatoes
- 2 pounds of white fish pieces
- 8 shrimp, medium
- 1/2 to 1 quart of seafood broth
- Salt, kosher, as desired

Instructions:

1. Toast blanched almonds in fry pan or under broiler. Chop leaves of parsley. Peel, then chop garlic.

2. Place garlic, almonds and parsley in food processor. Crumble stale bread. Add remainder of ingredients.

3. Process and mash ingredients as you add vinegar and oil slowly. Form a paste. Set it aside.

4. Peel and chop garlic and onion. Cube the tomatoes. Peel then slice potatoes into 1/4" thick rounds.

5. Pour several tbsp. oils in large sized fry pan. Heat over med. heat. Sauté onion for a couple minutes. Add garlic and tomatoes. Continue cooking. Add potatoes. Stir and coat well.

6. Mix several tbsp. of seafood broth with picada. Add to the pan. Simmer.

7. When potatoes have nearly cooked, add fish to the pan. Simmer. Add more broth if needed and thicken the sauce. When fish and potatoes have cooked, add the shrimp. Cook till shrimp are done and season as desired. Serve the soup hot.

9 – Spanish-Style Chicken

This recipe has travelled from the Catalan region of Spain to many countries. Many people remember eating it often when they were growing up, and for lots of those people, it's still a favorite.

Makes 6 Servings

Cooking + Prep Time: 1 1/2 hour

Ingredients:

- 1 cubed 3 – 3 1/2 lb. chicken, whole
- 2 cups of oil, olive

- 1/2 cup of melted butter, unsalted
- 1 head of minced garlic, roasted
- 1/4 cup of Spanish smoked paprika, sweet
- Salt, kosher, as desired
- Pepper, ground, as desired

Instructions:

1. Preheat the oven to 350F.

2. Place chicken pieces in roasting pan with the skin-side facing down. Pour butter and oil over chicken. Sprinkle with paprika and garlic. Season as desired.

3. Roast in 350F oven for 30-35 minutes. Turn chicken pieces with skin-side facing up. Roast till chicken is done cooking and skin turns crispy, usually 25-30 minutes more. Internal temperature should be 165F.

4. Serve chicken with sauce to dip in.

10 – Romesco Sauce

This delectable sauce is made with red peppers, olive oil, garlic and almonds. It is deceptively simple, since it can be paired with many dishes, to complete them deliciously.

Makes 8-10 Servings

Cooking + Prep Time: 15 minutes

Ingredients:

- 1/2 cup of almonds, roasted
- 1/2 cup of Parmesan cheese, grated
- 1 clove of garlic
- 1 1/2 oz. of drained red peppers, roasted
- 2 tbsp. oil, olive
- 1 tbsp. of vinegar, red wine
- Salt, kosher

Instructions:

1. Pulse garlic clove, almonds and Parmesan in food processor.

2. Add vinegar, oil, red peppers 1/4 tsp. kosher salt. Blend till smooth.

3. Serve with vegetables and bread.

11 – Broiled Mackerel

This simply-named recipe tells you exactly what it is. It's a delicious, quick and simple dish to make and tastes best if you have freshly caught fish.

Makes 6 Servings

Cooking + Prep Time: 20 minutes

Ingredients:

- 6 x 3-oz. Spanish mackerel fillets
- 1/4 cup of oil, olive

- 1/2 tsp. of paprika, sweet
- Kosher salt ground pepper, as desired
- 12 lemon slices, fresh

Instructions:

1. Preheat oven broiler. Set oven rack 6" from heat source. Grease baking dish lightly.

2. Rub each side of mackerel fillets with oil. Place with skin side facing down in baking dish. Season fillets with paprika, kosher salt ground pepper. Top fillets using lemon slices.

3. Bake fillets under broiler till fish starts flaking, about five to seven minutes and serve promptly.

12 – Catalan Calçots

Calçots may not sound like an easy recipe, but they are. You don't need to clean the vegetables or cut off their roots. Just place them on your BBQ grill. They cook best while the fire still has actual flames, not just embers.

Makes various # of servings depending on size

Cooking + Prep Time: 25 minutes

Ingredients:

- 1 bunch calçots
- Oil, olive
- Salt, kosher

- Romesco sauce, bottled

Instructions:

1. Preheat the oven to 475F. Peel off calçots' exterior layers. Rinse off any dirt that remains.

2. Set on oven tray. Drizzle them with oil. Sprinkle with kosher salt. Pop them into the oven. Rearrange them occasionally till calçots are tender and charred. Serve with the Romesco sauce.

13 – Spanish Potatoes

These tasty potatoes work well as a side dish with any barbequed meat, especially steaks. Top them with a couple hard-boiled egg slices for an authentic Catalan feast.

Makes 6 Servings

Cooking + Prep Time: 1 1/2 hour

Ingredients:

- 1/4 cup of oil, olive
- 1 thinly sliced onion, yellow

- 1 minced garlic clove
- 1 1/2 cups of sherry, dry
- 1 bay leaf, medium
- 4 x 1/2" thick peeled, sliced potatoes
- 1/4 cup of green onions, chopped
- 1/4 cup of minced parsley, fresh
- 1 tsp. of paprika, sweet
- Salt, kosher, as desired
- Pepper, ground, as desired

Instructions:

1. Heat the oil in large sized skillet on med. heat. Add garlic and onion. Stir while cooking till onion turns translucent, or about five to seven minutes. Add bay leaf and sherry and simmer till the flavors have combined, about six minutes.

2. Add potatoes. Cover the skillet. Stir occasionally while simmering till tender, 20-25 minutes.

3. Reduce the heat down to low. Discard the bay leaf. Add and stir paprika, green onions and parsley. Season as desired. Remove from the heat. Allow to cool down to room temp. and serve.

14 – Garbanzo Beans with Spinach

You can serve this recipe as a light meal or side dish. It goes especially well with crusty bread and grilled meats like pork chops.

Makes 4 Servings

Cooking + Prep Time: 1/2 hour

Ingredients:

- 1 tbsp. of oil, olive
- 4 minced garlic cloves

- 1/2 diced onion
- 1 x 10-oz. box of frozen, thawed, drained spinach, chopped
- 1 x 12-oz. can of drained garbanzo beans
- 1/2 tsp. of cumin, ground
- 1/2 tsp. of salt, kosher

Instructions:

1. Heat oil in skillet on med-low. Cook onion and garlic till translucent, five to six minutes.

2. Add and stir garbanzo beans, spinach, cumin and kosher salt. Mash beans lightly as the mixture is cooking. Allow them to cook till fully heated. Serve.

15 – Catalan Bell Pepper Stew

This hearty Catalan stew has juicy, rich flavors from many seasonal vegetables. The region has numerous vegetables grown in it, and there is always something tasty to include.

Makes 4 Servings

Cooking + Prep Time: 2 1/2 hours

Ingredients:

- 3 chopped garlic cloves
- 2 chopped onions, medium
- 1 diced bell pepper, green

- 1 diced bell pepper, red
- 5 peeled, de-seeded tomatoes, ripe
- 2 diced zucchinis
- 1/2 cup of oil, olive
- Salt, kosher
- Pepper, ground

Instructions:

1. Crush tomatoes.

2. Heat oil on med. heat in large sized Dutch oven. Lower heat. Brown onion and garlic for 12-15 minutes on low heat while regularly stirring.

3. Add bell peppers. Stir while cooking for 15 more minutes.

4. Add crushed tomatoes and zucchini. Season as desired.

5. Cover. Simmer over low heat for an hour and 35 minutes, stirring regularly and gently.

6. When cooked, remove lid. Increase heat a bit. Cook for 20 more minutes, till liquid evaporates.

7. Ensure that tomatoes remain juicy, but without retaining liquid from the rest of the vegetables. All ingredients should be incorporated well. Serve promptly.

16 – Tuna Avocado Tapas

Here is a healthy, light tapa that works well with crunchy bread and white wine. You can use this recipe to experiment, too, with different vegetables and spices.

Makes 4 Servings

Cooking + Prep Time: 25 minutes

Ingredients:

- 1 x 12-oz. can of water-packed, drained tuna, solid white
- 1 tbsp. of mayonnaise, reduced sodium
- 3 thinly sliced green onions + extra for garnishing
- 1/2 chopped bell pepper, red

- 1 dash of vinegar, balsamic
- Pepper, ground, as desired
- Garlic salt, as desired
- 2 halved, pitted avocadoes, ripe

Instructions:

1. Stir tuna, mayo, red pepper, green onions and vinegar together in medium bowl.

2. Season as desired. Pack avocado halves using tuna mixture.

3. Use reserved sliced green onions for garnishing and season with ground pepper. Serve.

17 – Catalan Squid and Rice

This dish is made in the Catalan and Valencian regions of Spain, using rice, prawns and squid. It's seasoned using complementary spices and herbs. You can purchase squid ink from fish dealers or buy it online.

Makes 3-5 Servings

Cooking + Prep Time: 1 3/4 hour

Ingredients:

- Oil, olive
- 1 finely diced onion, medium

- 1 stalk of celery, diced
- 2 bay leaves, medium
- 17 1/2 oz. of cleaned, dried, sliced squid
- 1 2/10 quarts of fish stock, light
- 4 x 4 gram sachets of squid ink
- 1 crushed clove of garlic
- 1 tsp. of paprika, smoked
- 1 bunch of chopped parsley, flat leaf
- 10 1/2 oz. of paella rice
- 4 1/4 fluid ounces of wine, white
- 8 king prawns, raw, whole
- 1/2 lemon, fresh

For aioli

- 1 egg yolk, large
- 4 1/4 fluid oz. of oil, olive
- 1 crushed clove of garlic
- 1 tbsp. of lemon juice, fresh
- 1 pinch pepper, cayenne

Instructions:

1. Heat 2 tbsp. of oil in large fry pan. Fry bay leaves, onion and celery for three minutes till they are soft. Add squid.

Cook over low heat for 18-20 minutes till squid becomes tender.

2. In a separate pan, heat fish stock. Add squid ink. Simmer gently.

3. Add garlic, 1/2 parsley, and paprika to squid. Fry for one more minute. Remove bay leaves and chop them finely before adding back to pan with rice. Stir till rice grains become coated with oil.

4. Add wine and briefly stir. Simmer for five to seven minutes. Add inky stock. Season well and simmer but do not stir. After 8-10 minutes, push prawns into rice. Cook till liquid has been absorbed, prawns are cooked, and rice is tender, about five to 10 more minutes.

5. To prepare aioli, put egg yolk in glass. Whizz with 1 tbsp. water and seasoning. Blend in oil a bit at a time till mixture has thickened and emulsified. Add and stir cayenne, garlic and lemon juice into mixture.

6. When rice has cooked fully, remove it from heat. Cover the pan. Allow it to rest for five to 10 minutes. Then scatter it with remaining parsley. Squeeze over the top with lemon. Serve with aioli.

18 – Sea Bass in Vinaigrette

Can't decide on how to best use a piece of tasty fish? Choose this crowd-pleasing, easy recipe that roasts seafood after slathering it in a wonderfully seasoned vinaigrette.

Makes 2 Servings

Cooking + Prep Time: 1/2 hour

Ingredients:

- 2 tbsp. of oil, olive + extra to drizzle
- 2 tbsp. of vinegar, sherry

- 1 tsp. of paprika, smoked, + extra to top
- 1 tsp. of salt, kosher + extra as desired
- 1/2 cup of green onions, sliced
- 1 sliced jalapeno pepper, red
- 4 small, quartered potatoes
- 2 x 8-oz. skinless, boneless, thick-cut sea bass fillets

Instructions:

1. Preheat the oven to 450F. Oil baking dish.

2. Microwave the potatoes in microwave-safe dish over high heat till barely softened, or about five to seven minutes.

3. Whisk vinegar and oil together in medium bowl. Add salt and paprika. Whisk and blend well. Stir in the cooked potatoes, onions and red jalapeno. Slide fish fillets into mixture. Turn and coat them with vinaigrette. Remove fish from the potato mixture.

4. Place the potatoes in the baking dish prepared above. Nestle the fish on potatoes. Sprinkle with 1 pinch salt, drizzle of oil and dash of paprika.

5. Bake in middle of 450F oven till cooked through, or about 15 minutes. Fish should flake easily. Serve.

19 – Catalan Pasta Paella

This dish is known as "Fideua" in the Catalan region, similar to traditional paella but it uses a short pasta that's like spaghetti. The fish stock with smooth pepper-tomato sauce adds to the flavors of seafood and fish.

Makes 4-6 Servings

Cooking + Prep Time: 55 minutes

Ingredients:

- 1 sea bass fillet with bones
- 1/2-pound of prawns/shrimp with shells still on

- 1 stalk of celery
- 1 small carrot, cleaned but unpeeled
- 2 parsley stems
- 1 thyme sprig
- 5 tbsp. +/- oil, olive
- 1 onion, Spanish
- 1 pepper, red
- 1/2 tsp. of paprika, sweet
- 3 garlic cloves
- 1/2 tsp. of fennel seeds
- 1 x 14-oz. can of tomatoes, crushed
- 15 +/- saffron threads
- 12 oz. of broken spaghetti or pasta
- 1/2 pound of clams

Instructions:

1. Remove shells from prawns/shrimp. Set shells aside.

2. Place fish bones, shrimp shells, carrot, celery, thyme sprig, parsley stems and small onion wedge in pot. Cover with water, about four cups. Bring pot to boil. Cover and reduce to simmer.

3. Chop remaining onion, garlic and pepper finely.

4. Heat 2 tbsp. oil in large sized fry pan on med-low. Fry shrimp and fish gently till nearly cooked through. Remove them from pan. Set them aside.

5. Clean out any bits and skin from the pan. Add remaining oil, then pepper and onion. Cook for about 10 minutes and stir occasionally. Add fennel seeds, paprika and garlic.

6. Strain stock created in step 2, removing all vegetables and bones. Infuse with saffron.

7. Cook onions in spice mixture for five minutes more. Add the tomatoes.

8. Cook for several more minutes. Add pasta. Stir completely, so pasta is covered by oil mixture. Cook for a couple more minutes.

9. Add stock to pan. Stir. Allow to simmer for 10 minutes.

10. Stir. Add clams and push them beneath pasta and liquid. Let them cook for a minute or two. Add fish, and prawns/shrimp. After five to seven minutes, clams will have opened and be ready. Serve.

20 – Spanish Sausage Chicken

This is a wonderful Catalan recipe that has been passed down through families for gatherings. It can be served for almost any event and works well with salad and bread.

Makes 6 Servings

Cooking + Prep Time: 1 hour

Ingredients:

- 1 tbsp. of oil, olive
- 1/2-lb. of sliced Italian sausage, sweet
- 1 x 8-oz. cubed chicken breast, skinless, boneless
- 1 chopped onion, medium
- 1 chopped bell pepper, medium
- 2 chicken bouillon cubes
- 1 2/3 cups of water, hot
- 1/2 tsp. of salt, kosher
- 1/2 tsp. of thyme, ground
- 1/4 tsp. of garlic powder
- 1 cup of green peas, frozen
- 1 1/2 cups of rice, instant
- 2 diced tomatoes, medium

Instructions:

1. Heat the oil in large sized skillet on med heat. Add and stir sausage in. Brown well, taking about five minutes. Remove sausage. Drain off the fat.

2. Stir the chicken, green pepper and onion into the skillet. Cook for five minutes.

3. Stir bouillon cubes in hot water in small sized bowl and dissolve them. Add and stir thyme, garlic powder and salt. Pour mixture into the skillet.

4. Add and stir peas into skillet. Bring to boil. Cover skillet. Reduce the heat down to med-low. Simmer for five or six minutes. Add and stir tomatoes and rice. Cover skillet. Remove it from the heat and allow to sit for five minutes. Serve.

21 – Fried Artichokes

You'll want to make more of these artichokes than you think you'll need, because once people start eating them, it's hard to stop. These are uniquely prepared artichokes and they go especially well with a beer.

Makes 4 Servings

Cooking + Prep Time: 1 1/4 hour

Ingredients:

For artichokes

- 6 artichokes, baby globe

- Salt, sea
- 1 squeeze lemon juice, fresh
- 1 cup of flour, all-purpose
- 2 ounces of corn starch
- 1 tsp. of baking powder
- 5 to 7 fluid ounces of water, sparkling
- To deep-fry: oil, olive

For alioli

- 1 1/2 oz. of membrillo
- 1 clove of garlic
- 1 egg yolk from large egg
- 2 tsp. of vinegar, white wine
- 1 pinch salt, sea
- 5 fluid ounces of oil, olive

Instructions:

1. Clean artichokes. Slice stem off a couple inches before base. Remove discard several outer leaves. Slice finely and place in bowl of water with a bit of lemon juice and salt.

2. Whisk baking powder and flour with sparkling water. You want a thick batter with no clumps. Drain artichokes. Par dry.

3. Heat oil in large sized pan to 350F. Dip sliced artichokes in batter. Drop them into oil. Fry for a couple minutes, till golden brown in color. Drain. Season using salt.

4. Mash membrillo garlic. Add vinegar and egg yolk and 1 pinch salt. Spoon into bowl. Whisk in oil gradually, forming glossy aioli. Serve with artichokes.

22 – Sherry Garlic Shrimp

You don't have to include lemon juice or sherry in this recipe, but it does add a wonderful contrast for the garlic and oil's rich taste. You can use scallops or squid instead of the shrimp too, if you like.

Makes 4 Servings

Cooking + Prep Time: 20 minutes

Ingredients:

- 4 minced garlic cloves
- 1/4 cup of oil, olive
- 1 tsp. of crushed pepper flakes, red
- 1 tsp. of paprika, smoked
- 1 lb. of peeled, de-veined shrimp, medium
- 2 tbsp. of sherry, dry or lemon juice, fresh
- Salt, kosher, as desired
- Pepper, ground, as desired
- 2 tbsp. of chopped parsley, flat leaf

Instructions:

1. Heat the garlic, oil, paprika and pepper flakes in large sized skillet on med-high.

2. Once oil has heated and garlic turned a golden brown color, raise heat up to high. Add shrimp. Cook till they turn opaque and pink, usually three or four minutes.

3. Deglaze pan with lemon juice or sherry. Season mixture as desired. Garnish with parsley and serve.

23 – Catalan Spinach

Normally, spinach is sautéed quickly. But in this tasty recipe, it is usually cooked for a longer period of time, cooking the spinach more thoroughly.

Makes 4 Servings

Cooking + Prep Time: 20 minutes

Ingredients:

- 4 peeled cloves of garlic
- 2 tbsp. of oil, olive
- 3 1/2 oz. of raisins

- 4 lbs. 6 oz. of spinach, baby
- 3 tbsp. of pine nuts
- Salt, sea pepper, ground

Instructions:

1. Heat oil in pan. Add garlic. Cook for a minute. Add pine nuts and raisins. Cook for one to two minutes, till pine nuts begin turning golden in color.

2. Add spinach. Sauté till well cooked and wilted. Season as desired. Serve.

24 – Catalan Vegetable Garlic Soup

This wonderful soup was made for me my first time by a person who actually runs a small restaurant in a town in Spain. After one bite, you'll be hooked, as I was.

Makes 6 Servings

Cooking + Prep Time: 50 minutes

Ingredients:

- 1 tbsp. of oil, olive
- 3 peeled, diced carrots, large
- 1 chopped cabbage head, medium

- 1/2 head of chopped cauliflower
- 2 sliced leeks
- 6 finely chopped garlic cloves
- 1 x 14 1/2 oz. can of tomatoes, diced, juice included
- 4 tsp. of tomato paste, low sodium
- 1 quart of water, filtered
- 1/4 cup of light cream or milk, 2%
- 1 tbsp. of butter, unsalted
- Salt, kosher pepper, ground, as desired

Instructions:

1. Heat the oil in large sized pot on med. heat. Add cabbage, carrot, leeks and cauliflower. Stir constantly while cooking for several minutes, till the cabbage has wilted.

2. Add and stir tomato paste and garlic. Continue cooking for another one to two minutes while constantly stirring, to prevent garlic from burning. Add and stir two cups of filtered water. Cover pan. Simmer for 8-10 minutes.

3. Next, pour in tomatoes and last 2 cups of filtered water. Return pot to boil. Reduce the heat down to low. Cover pot. Simmer for 18-20 minutes.

4. Reserve two cups of liquid. Puree the rest of the soup in food processor. Then return blended mixture to reserved liquid. Add and stir butter and milk. Return to boil. Cook for a minute or so. Season as desired. Serve.

25 – Lobster Rice

Catalan lobster recipes are especially tasty, with the local rice and other types of local ingredients used. This lobster and rice dish brings out the flavor of the lobster wonderfully.

Makes 8 Servings

Cooking + Prep Time: 1 1/4 hour

Ingredients:

- 2 x 1 pound 9 ounce lobsters
- 17 fluid ounces of stock, fresh shellfish

- 17 fluid ounces of stock, chicken
- 2 oz. of oil, olive
- 2 finely chopped onions, large
- 4 sliced cloves of garlic
- 1 1/3 cup of rice, short-grain
- 7 fluid ounces of wine, white
- 1 pound and 5 ounces of finely chopped tomatoes, fresh
- Salt, sea and pepper, ground
- Good sized pinch saffron threads
- 1 pound and 2 ounces of chunk-cut hake
- 1 pound and 2 ounces of cleaned clams, fresh

Instructions:

1. Use a heavy, sharp knife to halve lobsters down middle. Remove and discard stomachs. Remove claws. Crack with rolling pin or knife back. Remove small sized legs.

2. Combine both stock types in pan. Heat till they steam.

3. Heat oil in large pan. Fry onions gently for 10-12 minutes till they have softened. Add rice and garlic. Fry for one to two minutes till rice has toasted. Add tomatoes and wine.

Stir while cooking till mixture absorbs wine. Add saffron threads.

4. Pour 25 fluid ounces of hot stock into rice. Stir thoroughly. Season as desired. Nestle lobsters in rice. Gently cook with no stirring, for 12-15 minutes.

5. Add hake. Cook for three to five more minutes. Add clams and a splash of the stock. Cover. Cook for one to two minutes till clams have opened, discarding any that don't open. Serve with plenty of bread.

Like most European regions, Catalan has their own scrumptious desserts – try one soon!

26 – Catalan Churros

These churros are the Spanish version of Mexico's fried dough dessert. They are known all over the world for their deliciousness. They taste especially amazing when you sprinkle them with sugar or dip them in hot chocolate.

Makes 6 Servings

Cooking + Prep Time: 35 minutes

Ingredients:

For churros

- To fry: oil
- 1 cup of water, filtered
- 1 tbsp. of oil, vegetable
- 1/8 tsp. of salt, kosher
- 1 tsp. of sugar, granulated
- 1 cup of flour, white
- 1/4 tsp. of baking powder

For topping

- Honey or sugar, as desired

Instructions:

1. Pour the frying oil in large, heavy fry pan. Be sure you have two inches of oil in pan, so that churros are covered. They should freely float while they fry. Set pan aside.

2. Pour a cup of filtered water in medium sized sauce pan. Add 1 tbsp. oil, then sugar and salt. Stir well. Bring the water to boil.

3. Dry cup used for water measuring. Use it for measuring flour. Pour that flour in medium bowl. Add the baking powder. Stir.

4. Once water is boiling, remove sauce pan. Heat oil in fry pan.

5. Pour boiling water slowly from pan into flour mixture and stir constantly. You want a smooth dough that has no lumps. Dough should be smooth and sticky, not runny.

6. Spoon dough immediately into cookie press or a pastry bag.

7. Squeeze dough carefully into the heated oil. Fry till a golden brown in color. Remove from oil. Place on plate with paper towels for draining.

8. Cut into lengths that are manageable. Sprinkle with honey or sugar, as desired. Serve.

27 – Mel i Mató

This is very much a local Catalan dessert. It's made with a whole milk-based cheese that has a texture similar to ricotta, but a milder taste. The dish is especially tasty served with local honey.

Makes various servings depending on size of each

Cooking + Prep Time: 35 minutes + 2 hours chilling/draining time

Ingredients:

- 17 fluid ounces of milk, whole
- 1/2 lemon, juice only

- Honey, as desired
- Crushed nuts, pistachios, walnuts and pine nuts, as desired

Instructions:

1. In heavy sauce pan, bring milk to boil. Remove from heat.

2. Add lemon juice to hot milk. Stir thoroughly till it has curdled.

3. Line fine colander with cheese cloth. Press mixture through till all visible whey has drained off and all you have left is a simple lump of mato cheese.

4. Place colander over medium bowl. Keep in the refrigerator for two hours or so. This allows the excess water to drain and keeps the cheese chilled.

5. When you want to serve the dessert, add honey and nuts, as desired. Serve.

28 – Crumble Cakes

These traditional cakes, also called "mantecados", do indeed crumble easily. They are so light and soft in texture that they literally can melt in your mouth. You'll love them.

Makes 84 cookies

Cooking + Prep Time: 45 minutes

Ingredients:

- 1 cup of oil, vegetable
- 2 1/4 cups of shortening, vegetable

- 1 2/3 cups of sugar, granulated
- 4 egg yolks, large
- 2 shots anise
- 1 grated lemon peel
- 2 tbsp. of lemon juice, fresh
- 1/2 tsp. of cinnamon, ground
- 7 1/4 cups of flour, white, unbleached
- 1/2 tsp. of baking soda
- To beat for glaze: 1 egg white, large

Instructions:

1. Preheat the oven to 325F.

2. In large sized bowl, use hand mixer to whip oil and shortening together. Add sugar. Mix till smooth. Add anise, egg yolks, cinnamon, lemon peel and lemon juice. Mix well.

3. Add the flour one cup after another. Add the baking soda. Mix thoroughly. Dough should be soft and smooth.

4. Scoop out one dollop dough with teaspoon. Form balls roughly walnut-sized with your hands. Add extra flour if dough seems too sticky.

5. Place dough balls on cookie sheet. Press down on each ball lightly till they flatten a bit. Brush beaten egg white atop cookies. Bake till they start turning light brown around bottom edges, or 15-20 minutes.

6. Allow cookies to cool for about five minutes. Remove carefully from cookie sheet. Serve.

29 – Crema Catalana

Although this dish is compared sometimes to French crème brûlée, it is not as rich or heavy as the French dessert. It **Makes** a wonderful finish to a dinner of heavy paella.

Makes 4 Servings

Cooking + Prep Time: 1/2 hour + 2-3 hours chilling time

Ingredients:

- 4 egg yolks, large
- 1 cup of sugar, granulated
- 1 stick of cinnamon

- 1 lemon, zest only
- 2 cups of milk, whole
- 1 tbsp. of corn starch

Instructions:

1. Beat 3/4 cup of sugar with egg yolks in large pan till ingredients are blended thoroughly and mixture starts turning frothy.

2. Add lemon zest and cinnamon stick. Stir.

3. Add corn starch and milk. Heat mixture slowly and stir constantly, only till mixture starts thickening.

4. As soon as you can feel resistance from the mixture as you stir, remove pot from heat right away. Otherwise mixture could separate or curdle.

5. Remove cinnamon stick. Ladle milk mixture into four to six ramekins. Let them cool down to room temperature. Place in refrigerator for two to three hours.

6. Heat broiler. Remove ramekins from fridge. Sprinkle remaining sugar over them.

7. When broiler has heated, place ramekins under it on top shelf. Allow sugar to bubble and caramelize. It will turn a golden brown color. This could take between five and 10 minutes. Watch it closely so it doesn't burn. Remove. Serve promptly.

30 – Chocolate Turrón

This dessert is quite famous and quite popular. There are many varieties you can make, too. It's only found for sale around the Christmas holidays, but this recipe will let you make it whenever you like.

Makes 12 Servings

Cooking + Prep Time: 55 minutes

Ingredients:

- 5 oz. of blanched almonds, whole
- 2 oz. of pistachios, peeled
- 2 sheets of paper, wafer
- 7 oz. of honey, pure
- 7 ounces of sugar, superfine
- 1 egg white, large
- 1 tbsp. of cocoa powder

Instructions:

1. Preheat oven to 325F. Line cookie sheet. Roast nuts on sheet till light golden brown in color. Watch them closely, so they don't burn. Set them aside and allow them to cool.

2. Line a 7-inch square baking tin with one layer wafer paper.

3. Put sugar and honey in pan on low heat. Melt sugar. Bring mixture to rapid boil. Cook till it reaches 250F on sugar thermometer.

4. Beat egg white in stand mixer till it will hold soft peaks. While whisking, pour in hot honey and sugar mixture gradually.

5. When all are mixed well, scoop that mixture back into pan on med-low heat. Stir it constantly. You want to reduce its moisture content.

6. When mixture reaches 300 to 310F on sugar thermometer, begin to test it. Drop a small bit of it into cold water. It should immediately harden into a ball.

7. When the mixture tests well for hardening, add cocoa powder and nuts to it. Combine well. Pour into your lined tin. Smooth over. Top with another layer of the wafer paper. Allow to set before you slice and serve.

Conclusion

This Catalan cookbook has shown you…

…How to use different ingredients to affect unique Spanish tastes in dishes both well-known and rare. There are tastes that everyone will enjoy.

How can you include Catalan cooking in your home recipes?

You can…

- Make tomato toast, which nearly everyone in the region knows about. It is just as tasty as you may have heard.
- Learn to cook with canned and fresh tomatoes, which are widely used in Spain. Find them in the produce department of local food markets.
- Enjoy making the delectable seafood dishes of Spain, including salmon, mackerel and cod. Fish is a mainstay in the region, and there are SO many ways to make it great.
- Make dishes using eggplants and peppers, which are often used in Catalan cooking.

- Make various types of desserts like Chocolate Turrón and Crema Catalana that will tempt your family's sweet tooth.

Have fun experimenting! Enjoy the results!

Printed in Great Britain
by Amazon